PRAYERS
OF
THE
RIGHTEOUS

PRAYERS OF THE RIGHTEOUS

LAVERNE HAYES HARRIS

Published By Omega Publishing Co.

Copyright © 2016 by LaVerne Hayes Harris

published in the United States by Thomas Nelson, Inc.
Distributed by Omega Publishing Company
ISBN: 978-1533020987
Manufactured in the United States of America

Published Februry, 2016

Dedication

This book is dedicated to the prayer warriors and intercessors who pray without ceasing for God's people. Your love is shared through prayer and supplication. May you continue to stand strong with every spiritual and physical need met with Heaven's best.

Acknowledgements

Many thanks to Bishop I.V. Hilliard and Pastor Bridgett Hilliard for teaching the uncompromising Word of Truth shared in this book. You taught me to trust God's Word to accomplish all that it says it will.

Thank you to my dear friends and sisters, Amelia Young and Loretta Norris, for running to help me in this project. Once again you saw my vision and provided much needed support, companionship, guidance and encouragement. I could not have done it without you.

I offer a special thanks to God for entrusting me with this project and blessing me with the skills and talents to complete it. I am honored you chose me and I enjoyed writing with you.

TABLE OF CONTENTS

INTRODUCTION

Philippians 4:6-7 says "Do not be anxious about anything, but in everything by prayer and supplication with thanksgiving let your requests be made known to God. And the peace of God, which surpasses all understanding, will guard your hearts and your minds in Christ Jesus." (KJV)

God's Word instructs us to always pray for one another and for ourselves. Prayer is the channel by which we communicate and fellowship with God. It is a powerful medium which, when used accurately and effectively, brings great results. Prayer must be based upon God's Word. *"For the word that God speaks is alive and full of power—making it active, operative, energizing and effective; it is sharper than any two-edged sword, penetrating to the dividing line of the breath of life (soul) and (the immortal) spirit, and of joints and marrow (that is of the deepest parts of our nature) exposing and sifting and analyzing and judging the very thoughts and purposes of the heart"* (Hebrews 4:12, Amplified)

God's Word is our contact with Him. He instructs us to put Him in remembrance of His Word (Isaiah 43:26 KJV) and thereby place a demand on that Word to accomplish all that it says it will. (Isaiah 55:11 KJV)

1

We do not have to be ignorant of God's thoughts, His will or His purposes for our life. He left us His Word which provides all of the information necessary to live a victorious, overcoming life. .

The prayers in this book have been taken solely from the Word of God. They say what God says about every situation and circumstance. These prayers can be used to pray for yourself or for others. Each one is designed to be used interchangeably. As you pray each prayer, allow God's Word to settle down in your Spirit. Your Spirit will become alive to that Word and you will begin to think like God thinks and speak as God speaks. His ways and His statutes are not "mysterious". They are not difficult to discern because they are given through His Word.

It takes someone to pray; God requires that we pray. We also pray because we are commanded to. Psalm 100:4 says, *"Enter his gates with thanksgiving, and his courts with praise! Give thanks to him; bless his name!"* Thanking God, praising Him, and blessing Him are all aspects of prayer. There are many different kinds of prayers—the prayer of thanksgiving, the prayer of praise, the prayer of worship, and the prayer of supplication that changes things. All prayer is holy unto God and should be done without ceasing.
God has not left us helpless. We are instructed to take the Sword of the Spirit which is the Word of God and "Pray at all times—on every occasion, in every season, in the Spirit with all manner of prayer and entreaty. (Ephesians 6, Amplified)

The Word tells us that we are a tri-part being—we are spirit, we have a soul and we live in a physical body. Each part is necessary to the growth and development of the individual and must be fed properly. The soul which is the intellectual part of man must be fed intellectual food. The body must be fed physical food and the spirit must be fed spiritual food which is the Word of God.

The purpose of this book is to provide your Spirit man with the spiritual food it needs to develop spiritually. We must allow ourselves to grow in the things of God by feeding ourselves large portions of God's Word daily. As God told Joshua, "...*thou shalt meditate therein (on this word) day and night, that thou may observe to do according to all that is written therein; for then thou shalt make thou way prosperous and then thou shalt have good success.*" (Joshua 1:8 KJV) Prayer is spending time with God, learning his wisdom, basking in His Love.

I WILL PRAISE YOU WITH MY WHOLE HEART

It is always appropriate to begin your prayer session with praise to God. Below are prayers of praise.

1. We sing praises unto you Lord for you are the rock of our salvation. We come before your presence with thanksgiving, and make a joyful noise unto you with psalms; for You are a great God, and a great King above all gods. In your hands are the deep places of the earth and the strength of the hills . The sea is yours, You made it:. Your hands formed the dry land. I worship and bow down to you:. I kneel before you O Lord. O God our maker. Amen

2. Blessed be thou, Lord God of Israel our father, for ever and ever. You, O Lord are great and mighty. You are powerful, and glorious, victorious, and majestic. All that is in the heaven and in the earth is yours. I exhalt your kingdom, O Lord, and thou art exalted as head above all. Both riches and honor come of thee, and thou reigns over all. In Your hand is power and might; to make great, and to give strength unto all. Now therefore, our God, we thank thee, and praise thy glorious name.

3. O Lord, Our God. You are Wisdom -- You are Truth. You handle the mighty, and You look after the weak. You make sense out of our struggles, and You shine a light on all our broken parts. You promise healing and You restore the lost. Everything got started in You and finds its purpose in You. You will not be ignored, and You will not leave us alone to struggle in our selfishness. I look at You and acknowledge Your Presence, and I shout praises of thanksgiving.

4. Jesus, You are highly exalted, and Your name is above every name! We ask all of our prayers in Your name Jesus. Your name is above the name of all sicknesses and diseases. Your name is above depression, and poverty, and all other names. Blessed be Your name Lord! You are the solution to any problem, and You are bigger than any obstacle we face.

5. I will praise You, O LORD, with my whole heart; I will show forth all Your marvelous works. I will be glad and rejoice in You: I will sing praise to Your name, O thou most High. Let the words of my mouth, and the meditation of my heart, be acceptable in Your sight, O LORD, my strength, and my redeemer.

6. Let my mouth be filled with Your praise and with Your honor all the day. O LORD our Lord, how excellent is thy name in all the earth! You are Emmanuel, God with us. You are a Wonderful, Counselor, The mighty God, The everlasting Father, The Prince of Peace. We praise You Lord! You are unlimited, almighty, all-powerful, and all-knowing. You are the Alpha and Omega, the beginning and the end. The First and the Last. You are the King of Kings & Lord of Lords! You are the true and living God.

7. Father, I praise You for being Jehovah Jireh, my provider; Jehovah Rapha, my healer; Jehovah Nissi, my banner; Jehovah Mckaddesh, my santification; Jehovah Shalom, my peace; Jehovah Tsidkenu, my righteousness; Jehovah Shammah, my ever present help; Jehovah Rohi, my guide and Jehovah Elohim, my God.

8. I will worship toward thy holy temple, and praise thy name for thy lovingkindness and for thy truth: for thou hast magnified thy word above all thy name.

Scripture References:

Psalms 95: 1-6
I Chronicles 29:10
Psalms 34:3
Proverbs 2:6
Psalms 19:14
Psalm 9:1
Psalms 19:14
Isaiah 9:6
Psalms 138:2
Revelations 22:13
Psalms 63:3
Genesis 22:14
Exodus 15:26
Judges 6:24
Jeremiah 33:16

PRAYER TO BE MORE SPIRITUALLY MINDED

Father, I thank You that I am created in Your likeness. I am a child of God, born of the Spirit, filled with Your Spirit, and led by Your Spirit.

I thank You that the Holy Spirit is guiding me into all truth. I believe I have the mind of Christ and I hold the thoughts and purposes of His heart. Wisdom and knowledge is pleasing to me and I continually seek to be more spiritually directed.

The Holy Spirit is my comforter and my guide and comes to give direction and illumination to my mind. He leads me in the way I should go, ordering my footsteps and guiding my path. Because I am sensitive to His voice, I have ears to hear and the eyes of my understanding are enlightened.

Guide me in your truth, O Lord, and teach me your decrees, for you are my Savior and my hope is in you all day long. Teach me your way and lead me the way I should go. I trust in the Lord with all my heart and all my mind and I lean not to my own understanding. In all my ways I will acknowledge Him and He will direct my path.

The Word of God shall not depart out of my mouth. I will meditate therein day and night. Therefore I will make my way prosperous and have good success in all that I do. I will evermore praise you with the voice of thanksgiving and tell of your wondrous works. In Jesus name. Amen

Scripture References

Genesis 1:27
John 3:6
John 14:16, 26
John 16:13
I Corinthians 2:16
Proverbs 2:10
Proverbs 3:5-6
Joshua 1:8
Psalms 119:64
Psalms 25:5
Psalms 26:7

PRAYER TO LIVE A LIFE PLEASING TO GOD

Father, I thank You that Your Word is a lamp unto my feet and a light unto my pathway — going forth to accomplish all that it is sent unto. Through that Word, I am able to hear the voice of the Good Shephard and the voice of a stranger I will not follow.

Father, I pray that the words of my mouth and the meditations of my heart are acceptable in your sight. You are my rock and my redeemer. My desire is to walk in a manner that is pleasing to you Lord. Jesus has made unto me wisdom and I single-mindedly walk in that wisdom expecting to know what to do in every situation, on top of every circumstance.

I roll my works upon you Lord and You make my thoughts agreeable to Your will. I I thank You that I am able to perceive and recognize more strongly and clearly what I am to do. My desire is to please you in all things, bearing fruit in every good work. I stand firm and mature in spiritual growth convinced and fully assured in everything willed by God as I become more intimately acquainted with your will.

I thank you Father for the Holy Spirit who abides permanently in me and who guides me into all truth,

9

and speaks to me whenever He hears from the Father and announces the things that are to come. I have the mind of Christ and I hold the thoughts, feelings, and purposes of His heart. I believe in my heart and I say with my mouth that this day the will of God is done in my life as I daily live a life that is pleasing to You Lord.

Scripture References

Psalm 19:14
John 16:13
John 10:27
I Corinthians 9:10
James 1:5-8
Hebrews 4:10
John 16:13
Ephesians 5:17
Colossians 1
Acts 22:14

PRAYER FOR DIVINE FAVOR

I thank You Lord God that You are my sun and shield; You give grace and glory. You promise that no good thing will be held from them that walk up rightly. You are a gracious God, kind and merciful always giving favor.

I thank You Father that I am a success this day and I find favor with You and man. I am the head and not the tail, above only and not beneath. Lord Jesus, I humble myself before You and I ask that You grant me favor today as I _____ (be specific in naming the place or situation in which you need favor).

Open the hearts of those whom I will speak with this day and cause them to receive me positively. Let the words of my mouth and the meditations of my heart be acceptable in Your sight my rock and my redeemer. I pray that what I am requesting favor for is within Your perfect will for my life. I thank you that you are doing exceedingly, abundantly, above all that I could ask or think according to the power that works within me. May my prayers open the storehouse of your blessings. The peace of God rules my heart and I will not worry about anything. I am complete in You Father and favor follows me today. In Jesus name. Amen

Scripture References

Psalm 84:11
Deuteronomy 28:18
Psalm 19:14
Malachi 3:10
II Peter 3:18
Proverbs 3:4
Ephesians 3:20

Special Prayer Requests

PRAYER TO REQUEST FORGIVENESS FROM SIN

Father, Your Word says that if we confess our sins You are faithful and just to forgive us our sins and to cleanse us from all unrighteousness. I therefore take this opportunity to confess that I am a sinner and to ask that you forgive me. Your Word says that I am redeemed through the blood of Jesus and that I receive forgiveness of sins according to the richness of Your grace.

I thank You Father for forgiving me and I receive that forgiveness right now. I make a renewed commitment to you and I submit my life to your service. From this moment on, I will walk in love, seek peace and conduct my life in a manner pleasing to you. I will love my enemies, do good, and lend hoping for nothing. When I do this your Word says that my reward will be great and I shall be a child of the Highest.

It is written in Your Word that the love of God has been shed abroad, poured forth into my heart by the Holy Ghost who was given freely to all men. I believe that God's love which is in me flows into the lives of everyone I know. The fruit of righteousness now abounds in my life and brings glory and honor to You Lord in Jesus name. Amen

Scripture References

I John 1: 9
Colossians 1:14
Ephesians 4:31
Ephesians 1:7
Luke 6:35
Romans 5:5

Special Prayer Requests

PRAYER FOR EMPLOYMENT

Father, Your Word says that I can have confidence that when I pray according to Your Word and Your will for my life I know that I have the petitions that I desire. Because I desire to owe no man nothing but to love him, I thank you that the labor of my hands is blessed and I gain employment at the highest level possible for me.

I thank You Father that You are raising up someone to use their power, their ability, and their influence to help me. My wages will not be counted as favor or a gift but as something owed to me. I commit to perform good deeds, through honest employment so that I am able to meet every need in abundance. Your Word says that you give seed to the sower. I dedicate my financial seeds from gainful employment so that I can pay my bills, give to the kingdom and live the abundant life Jesus came to provide.

Satan, you are bound from interfering in this situation. I will not fret or have anxiety over anything, for Your peace, Father, guards my heart and mind. You are doing exceeding, abundantly above all that I could ever ask or think. You direct and make straight my path while opening doors that can never be closed. I thank You Father that my employment and promotions come speedily. In Jesus name. Amen

Scripture references

I John 5:15
Romans 3:18
Psalm 128:2
Romans 4:4
II Corinthians 9:10
Philippians 4:7
Ephesians 3:20
Proverbs 3:6

Special Prayer Requests

PRAYER FOR PROTECTION

Father, your name is a strong tower and I know I can run to You and find safety. You shall preserve me from evil. You preserve my going out and my coming in from this time and even for evermore.

Thank You for being my refuge and my fortress. I choose to dwell in the secret place of the most High and abide under the shadow of the Almighty. There I find safety and ease. When I lie down, I will not be afraid. I will lay down in peace and sleep for thou, O Lord, maketh me to dwell in safety.

Father, I will not be afraid of evil tidings. I walk with confident trust in you. My heart and mind are kept in perfect peace because my mind remains fixed on your promises.

Thank you for giving your angels charge over me to guard me in all my ways . Satan and his principalities and powers that rule the present darkness and all spiritual wickedness in high places are turned back from any assignment against me or my family. No evil shall befall me nor any plague come near my dwelling. I will not be afraid of the terror by night nor the arrow that flieth by day for Your eyes are over the righteous and under Your wings I am covered and protected. The whole armor of truth, righteousness, peace. salvation, faith and God's Word covers and protects me. In Jesus name. Amen

Scripture References

Psalms 121:7
Proverbs 3:23-24
Psalms 91:1
Isaiah 26:3-4
Psalms 112:7
Psalms 91:10
Proverbs 18:10
Psalms 4:8
Ephesians 6: 13-17

Special Prayer Requests

PRAYER FOR HEALTH AND HEALING

"(Glory to Him) ..who in his own self bear our sins in his own body on the tree, that we being dead to sin should live unto righteousness; by whose stripes we were healed."

Thank You, Father, for Your Word concerning healing. We believe Your word will not return to You void of power but will accomplish everything that it is sent to do. Jesus bore every sickness, infirmity and disease on the cross for me. We pray in accordance with the holy scriptures and with great confidence we say that_____is healed in his/her whole body. They are redeemed from the curse of sickness and death and they refuse to tolerate its symptoms in their body.

Father, I speak to_____body and command every nerve, cell, organ, bone and muscle to function as it was designed. I declare that pain, disease and discomfort are far from them.

Satan, in the name of Jesus you can no longer continue to operate in the body of _____. You and your principalities and powers who rule the present darkness and your spiritual wickedness in heavenly places are bound. God's Word declares that whatever we bind in earth shall be bound in heaven.

19

Your assignment against_____is broken. His heart is established and shall not be afraid of evil tidings. His heart is fixed trusting in the Lord.

We declare that_____body is the temple of the Holy Spirit so we speak to that body and command that_____be healed and made whole in the name of Jesus and by the authority of God's Word. Amen

Scripture References

I Peter 2:24
Isaiah 55:11
James 4:7
II Corinthians 10:3
Psalms 112:7
I Corintiians 6:19

Special Prayer Requests

PRAYER FOR SALVATION

Father. I know that without you I am lost. I ask You to come into my life and save me. Your Word says that if I confess with my mouth that Jesus is Lord and believe in my heart that You raised Him from the dead, then I shall be saved. So right now, on the basis of that written Word I confess my desire to make Jesus my Lord and I believe that he died and was raised to ever live with God. I give You Lord the reigns to my life and I commit to serve You all the rest of my days.

Satan, you have no place in my life. I bind every corrupting spirit and say that I am now a child of the King. In Jesus Name. Amen.

Scripture References

Luke 19:10
I Timothy 2:1
Matthew 18:18
Romans 10:9
II Timothy 2:26
I Timothy 2:3

PRAYER TO BE FILLED WITH THE HOLY SPIRIT

"Behold, I will pour my spirit out to you, I will make known my words unto you."

Heavenly Father, You promised in Your Word that You would send another Comforter, the Holy Spirit, when I receive Jesus as my Lord and Savior. I confess Jesus is Lord and now I ask that You fill me with Your Spirit. I thank You Holy Spirit for coming into my life and making intercession for me according to the will of God. I receive your covenant promise, Oh Lord, to put Your words in my mouth which will not depart out of the mouth of my seed nor out of the mouth of my seed's seed henceforth and forever. In Jesus name. Amen.

Scripture References

Proverbs 1:23
Acts 1:8
I Corinthians 14
Isaiah 59:21
Ephesians 1:17
John 14:16

PRAYER TO GUARD MY TONGUE

Father, I believe that Your words are spirit and life so I choose to let them dwell in me richly in all wisdom. I therefore dedicate my mouth to speak excellent and princely things and the opening of my lips for right things.

I thank You that I have been made the righteousness of God through Jesus Christ. So I set the course of my lips for abundance, for wisdom, for health, for joy and for peace. I want the words of my mouth and the meditations of my heart to be acceptable in your sight O Lord, my strength and my redeemer. I guard my mouth and my heart with all diligence and I refuse to give Satan any place in me.

Father, today I commit to turn from idle words and foolish talk. Your word says that death and life are in the power of the tongue. I thank You that no corrupt communication shall proceed out of my mouth, only that which is edifying and a blessing to the body of Christ.

I recognize that my world is created by the words of my mouth. The ability of God is released within me by what I say. My words are alive in me and produce good things in my life and the lives of others. So I can

PRAYERS OF THE RIGHTEOUS

boldly say that my words are words of faith, words of power, words of praise and words of life.

Help me to use my words to edify others and impart grace to those who hear me. Give me words to speak in due season and let my words bring joy and not pain, life and not death, blessing and not cursing. Give me boldness to speak the truth of Your righteousness and tenderness to do so in love. Empower me by Your Holy Spirit to be your witness. Give me an ear to hear what Your Spirit would have me speak. Because I choose Your words for my lips, I also choose Your will for my life. In Jesus Name . Amen

Scripture References

Proverbs 8:6
John 6:63
Psalm 141:3
John 6:63
Psalm 19:14
Proverbs 18:21
Proverbs 15:23
Ephesians 4:15
Romans 1:18
Acts 1:8

PRAYER TO CAST OUT FEAR

Father, in the name of Jesus, I thank You and praise Your holy name. I thank You for who You are. You are my strength, my refuge and I confidently put my trust in you. I believe the wisdom of God dwells in me and I do not dread or fear. My mind , thought life and body is covered by the blood of Jesus and no hurt, harm nor torment shall affect me in any way.

In the name of Jesus I boldly come against the Spirit of fear. I bind up the attack of the enemy to torment my mind. I thank You all demonic assignments are cancelled that have been placed on my life. I boldly command Satan and his demons back to the pit of hell from whence they came with the full authority of the blood of Jesus promised to me through our covenant with God.

The Word says because You love me, You will rescue me. You will contend with that which contends with me. You said when I call , You will answer. You will be with me in trouble and promised to rescue me in times of distress. You satisfy me with a full life and give me salvation. So I choose, through an act of faith, to believe Your Word and put my trust in You that in my time of trouble I have confidence that You will protect me.

Now Father, I thank You that Your perfect love casts out all fear and the freedom from fear manifests now. So I boldly, say the Lord is my helper and I will not fear. No weapon formed against me shall prosper and every tongue that rises against me in judgement shall be shown to be in the wrong. I am far from oppression and fear does not come near me. In Jesus name. Amen

Scripture References

Psalms 91:10
Isaiah 54:17
Psalms 46:1
Hebrews 13:6
Isaiah 49.25
Psalms 91:2
Isaiah 54:14

26

PRAYER TO CAST OUT WORRY AND DOUBT

Father, because I dwell in the secret place of the Most High and abide under the shadow of the Almighty, you cover me. I cast the whole of my cares— all my anxieties, all my worries, all my concerns, all my doubts once and for all upon You. You perfect that which concerns me. You sustain me. You will never allow the consistently righteous to be moved or made to slip, fall or fail.

I thank, You Father that You are able to keep that which I have committed to You. I choose to think on those things that are true, honest, just, pure, lovely, of good report, virtuous and deserving of praise . I will let not my heart be troubled or allow doubt to rise. I will abide in your words and allow your words to abide in me.

Father, I will be careful for nothing but in everything with prayer and supplication I will let my requests be known unto You. And the peace of God which passes all understanding will keep my heart and mind from worry. My confidence is in You, O Lord. You have promised to answer me whenever I call, to be with me in trouble, and to deliver me from evil. You are my refuge and strength , therefore I will lay aside every weight and the sin of worry which does try so easily to affect me. I will run my race with patience looking unto Jesus, the author and finisher of my faith. In Jesus name. Amen

Scripture references

Romans 8:2
Hebrews 12:1
Colossians1:13
I Peter 5:6
II Timothy 1:12
John 14:1
John 15:7
James 1:22
Psalm 37:4
Psalm 138:8
Philippians 4:6
Psalm 46:1

Special Prayer Requests

PRAYER TO BLESS THE CHILDREN

Father, Your word says children are a gift from God and the fruit of the womb is Your reward. I believe the word and I thank You for entrusting these precious children to my care. I pray that You will grant them complete knowledge of Your will and bless them with all spiritual wisdom and understanding.

I confess that each day my children grow in wisdom and statue and find favor with God and man. They obey their father's commands and do not neglect their mother's teaching. Thank You that my children are wiser than the children of the world and they excel in all that they put their hands to do. My children are disciples taught of the Lord, obedient to His Word so great is their peace and undisturbed composure.

Father, I declare that no temptation shall overtake my children. I pray that You will guard their hearts and minds from the evil one. Angels of the Lord encamp around my children to protect them from all harm. I commit and cast the care of my children once and for all on You. I will train my children in the way they should go so that when they are old they will not depart from it. They are in Your hands and I am totally persuaded that You are more than able to keep that which I have committed to You. You are their shield and their fortress. You are more than enough.

O Lord, how excellent is thy name in all the earth. You have set Your glory above the heavens and have demonstrated Your strength to our enemies. My children and I will sing praise to Your Holy name. O Most High. Amen

Scripture References

Psalm 8:1-2
Isaiah 54:13
Proverbs 22:6
Colossians 1:9
Luke 2:52
Proverbs 6:20
Philippians 4:7
Isaiah 49.25
Psalm 91:2

Special Prayer Requests

PRAYER FOR PARENTS

Father, I submit myself to You. I realize that as a parent I need Your direction in order to raise my children as You would have me to. I therefore want to partner with You and partake of Your gifts of wisdom, discernment, revelation, and guidance. I need Your strength, Your patience and Your love. Where I need to be healed, delivered, changed, matured or made whole, I invite You to do that in me. Help me to walk in righteousness and integrity before You. Teach me Your ways, enabled me to obey Your commandments and do what is pleasing in Your sight.

As a parent I will not provoke, irritate or fret my children. I will not cause them to become discouraged, saddened or made to feel inferior. I will not break their will or wound their spirit but will rear them in the fear and admonition of the Lord. I will train them in the way they should go and when they are old they will not depart from it.

May the beauty of Your spirit be evident in me so that I will be a Godly example for my children. Teach me to touch them with Your hands –gentle but firm and caring. Teach me to talk to them with Your lips –speaking uncompromised truth. Teach me to love them with Your love –unconditional and everlasting.

Help me to show honor to You by being a blessing and a good parent to the children You have entrusted to my care. In Jesus Name. Amen

Scripture References

Exodus 31:3
Proverbs 8:20
Psalms 25:14
Ephesians 5:10
Proverbs 22:6

Special Prayer Requests

PRAYER TO BLESS
A MARRIAGE

Father, we thank You that as husband and wife we walk worthy of You Lord--pleasing You, being fruitful in every good work and increasing in the knowledge of God. We commit to being immitators of You, following Your example, esteeming , delighting and loving one another as Christ loved us.

As husband and wife we will be gentle, compassionate, courteous, tender hearted, and kind. We will not be boastful or display ourselves haughtily. We will not be rude or selfish or act unbecomingly. We believe that with our minds and hearts guided by You our marriage will be peaceful and our prayers will not be hindered in any way. We are heirs together of the grace of God.

We thank You Father because our marriage is rooted and grounded in Your love it grows stronger every day. We commit ourselves to live in mutual harmony, on one accord, delighting in each other, being of the same mind and united in spirit. We will be forgiving of one another even as God, for Christ's sake has forgiven us. We vow to live in harmony with one another, to be sympathetic, compassionate and humble.

Satan, we render you helpless in our lives and come against your spirit of divorce and separation. What God has joined together shall not be torn apart.

Thank You our marriage is blessed. In Jesus name. Amen

Scripture References

Colossians 1:10
Ephesinas 5:1
I Corinthians 13:14
I Peter 3:7
Romans 15:5

Special Prayer Requests

PRAYER FOR FINANCIAL INCREASE

Father, we thank You that Your Word is a lamp unto our feet and a light onto our pathway. We confess that You are able to make all grace abound toward us, every favor and earthly blessing comes to us in abundance. Christ has redeemed us from the curse of poverty sickness and death. We thank You that in all situations and circumstances, whatever the need, we have all sufficiency in all things such that every need is met.

Your word teaches to give and it shall be given to us-- good measure, pressed down, shaken together should men give into our bosom. Because I have given to further Your gospel in the earth so that Your church is established, I therefore confess a 100 fold return on my giving. With the same measure I give is the same measure by which I receive. If I give bountifully, I will reap bountifully.

We thank You Father that You have released ministering spirits which are now free to bring in the necessary financial increase. We praise You in advance for sudden breakthroughs like the bursting out of great waters and that all hindrances to our blessings all removed. Every financial need is met in abundance. In Jesus name. Amen

Scripture References

Psalms 119:105
II Corinthians 9:8
Luke 6:38
Mark 10;29
II Samuel 5:30
Galatians 3:13

Special Prayer Requests

PRAYERS OF DELIVERANCE
(From Satan & Forces of Evil)

Father we realize that we wrestle not against flesh and blood but against principalities and powers, against the rulers of darkness and spiritual wickedness in high places. We thank You that You have equipped us to defeat Satan and the forces of evil. So we come confidently and boldly to You and present _____. Your Word says that when two or more agree about anything, they can ask what they will and it will be done by our Father which is in heaven. We, as brothers and sisters in the faith agree that_____is delivered from the evil that attempts to hold them in bondage. We, with our faith do break the hold of the enemy from his/her life.

Your Word says that whatsoever we bind on earth shall be bound in heaven. We therefore bind Satan in all of his maneuvers against_____. We speak to you, Satan, and all of your demonic forces and take authority over you and command you to flee from _____. You are a spoiled and defeated foe. We overcome by the Word which says when we resist the devil, he must flee from us.

Father we now plead the blood of Jesus over _____ life and call those things that be not as though they were. We declare that_____is unwrapped and set free from all evil influences.

I ask, Lord God, that You fill those vacant places in _____ with Your spirit, Your love, Your wisdom, Your righteousness and Your peace.

I thank You father that the angels of the Lord camp around and about_____ to help and assist. We declare that every enslaving yoke is broken. In Jesus name. Amen

Scripture References

Ephesians 6: 9-10
Matthew 18:19
Matthew 18:18
I John 3:8
John 11:11
Revelations 12:11
Romans 4:17
James 4:7

(From Destructive Habits)

Heavenly Father, I confidently put my trust in You. You are my strong tower and the defender of my soul. I believe all things work together for my good because of my love for You. You are perfecting all that concerns me so from this day forward, I confess that I am delivered from the habit(s) of _____.

I recognize that I wrestle not against flesh and blood but against principalities and powers, spirits who rule the present darkness and spiritual wickedness in high places. I thank You Lord that Satan is bound from me and no longer can operate against me. I have put on the whole armor of God so that I can destroy the works of the devil. The habit(s) of _____ are far from me and will no longer rule my life. I receive complete and total freedom Now, in Jesus name.

I thank you, Father that through Your Word I am strengthed in my inner self with Your mighty power to withstand all attacks and resist all temptations. I am able to discipline my body and control my flesh. I renew my mind daily with the Word of God, casting down imaginations and every thing that exalts itself over the knowledge of God. I bring into control every thought to make it obedient to Christ. I am set free because greater is He that is in me than he who is in the world. In Jesus name. Amen

Scripture References
Psalm 63:1
Romans 8:28
Ephesians 6: 11-12
Colossians 1:11
Romans 12:2
I Corinthians 10:5

A PRAYER FOR OUR SCHOOLS

Father, we bring the _____ school system before You and thank You that the men and women who are in authority are filled with skillful and godly wisdom and Your knowledge is pleasant to them. Their steps are ordered and they are directed by You so that they can do what is good and right in Your sight. We believe that they are men and women of integrity, who are obedient to Your word. Understanding keeps them and delivers them from the ways of evil and evil men. Father, we thank You that born again, spirit-filled men and women are in positions of authority having control of our school. The ungodly are cast out in the name of Jesus.

We thank You that the teachers and administrators commit to train our children in the way they should go so that when they are old, they shall not depart from it. We, therefore, believe that the children will develop their minds, body and spirit as they attend the _____ school system. They will show themselves to be blameless, guileless, innocent and uncontaminated children of God without blemish in the midst of a wicked generation. They will be wiser than the children of the world and find favor with their teachers and administrators.

Satan, we speak to you, the principalities and powers, the rulers of darkness and all wicked spirits in heavenly places. You are bound from operating against the _____ school system. We bind every spirit of the occult, every familiar spirit of witchcraft; we bind sexual immorality, obscenity, spirits of addiction; every disruptive, deceitful, violent spirit that would seek to infiltrate this school system. You are loosed from operating against the _____ school system in any way. Your assignment is broken. We commission ministering spirits to go forth and police the grounds, building, and walls of _____ school system dispelling the forces of darkness.

Thank You Father, that You are our deliverer, our protector, our guide. Thank You that the good news of the gospel is spread throughout this school system and all in authority carry out Your will and Your purpose. They walk in the light as You are the light. In Jesus name. Amen

Scripture References

Psalms 25:21
Proverbs 2:10
Galatians 5:20
Hebrews 1:14
Psalms 91:11
I John 1:7

A PRAYER FOR OUR GOVERNMENT

Heavenly father, I give thanks for our government. I pray for all men and women that have authority over us in any way. I pray for the President, the representatives, the senators, the governors, the policemen and judges of our land. Pour out Your Spirit upon them and make Your Word known to them. Cause them to be men and women of integrity, obedient concerning us, that we may lead a quiet and peaceable life in all godliness and honesty. Let wisdom enter their hearts and knowledge be pleasant to them. We thank You that their hearts and ears are attentive to godly counsel' doing what is right in Your sight.

We pray Father, that You cut off the wicked and let the unfaithful be rooted out. Let the upright dwell in our government. Let discretion preserve them and understanding keep them to deliver them from the way of evil and from evil men.

We thank You that You raise up a standard in this nation causing the reins of Your Spirit to flood this land. Raise up intercessors for this nation to pull down strongholds over this land. Let the Glory of the Lord be revealed for blessed is the nation whose God is the Lord. In Jesus name. Amen.

Scripture References

I Timothy 2:1-2
Proverbs 1:23
Psalms 25:21
Proverbs 2:10-11
Proverbs 2:21
Isaiah 49:22
Zechariah 10:1
Isaiah 40:5

Special Prayer Requests

A PRAYER FOR ISRAEL

Father, You are the God of Israel and they are Your people. We pray that You cleanse them from their iniquities and forgive them of all their sins. Raise them up in righteousness, save them with an everlasting salvation and direct all of their ways. Redeem Israel from their troubles. Be a shelter for Your people and the strength of the children of Israel. May the eyes of their understanding be enlightened. Give them the Spirit of wisdom and revelation in the knowledge of our Lord Jesus Christ.

We thank You Father that You restore everything that has been removed from them . Make their enemies to be at peace with them and no longer let them be a reproach among the nations.

We pray for the peace of Jerusalem. May they prosper that love You. Cause showers of blessings to come down in their season. May Your people dwell in safety in their land. Let Israel be to You a name of praise and honor before all nations of the earth. In Jesus name. Amen

Scripture References

Isaiah 45:3-4
Jeremiah 45:4
Isaiah 45: 13,17
Psalms 25:22
Ephesians 1:17
Jeremiah 33:9
Joel 2:25
Psalms 122:6
Ezekiel 34:26

Special Prayer Requests

CONTACT US

Our goal is to make this book available to as many people as possible. If you have family or friends whom you feel would benefit from the information shared herein, please contact us for additional copies.

Contact Information:

Omega Publishing Co.
6635 Cloud Swept
Houston, Texas 77086
281-794-5755
laverne@laverneharris.com
http/:www.laverneharris.com

Made in the USA
Monee, IL
06 July 2020

35819304R00033